A LETTER

TO THE

HON. GEORGE E. BADGER,

IN RELATION TO THE

CLAIM OF A. & J. E. KENDALL

AGAINST

THE UNITED STATES, FOR CERTAIN WRONGS DONE THEM,

WITH AN APPENDIX.

BY AMOS KENDALL.

WASHINGTON, D. C.
BUELL & BLANCHARD, PRINTERS.
1852.

LETTER.

WASHINGTON, *November* 13, 1852.

Hon. George E. Badger:

SIR: It is not in a spirit of disrespect that I address you. On the contrary, it is under the conviction that you are a man who does not wittingly let prejudice or partiality influence you in the performance of your duties, public or private; who has none of that foolish pride which prompts many to persist in error, though convinced; a man as ready to repair unintentional wrong as to maintain undoubted right.

Having this confidence in your integrity of purpose, and equal confidence in your ability to understand and give due weight to the law and the testimony, I proceed to show, or attempt to show, that you unwittingly did great injustice to myself and partner in your remarks in the Senate, at their late session, on our claim for services rendered the Western Cherokees.

It seems necessary, before we comment on those remarks, to state the law as it existed when we undertook the service, as also the facts of the case, and show the bearings of the one upon the other.

THE LAW OF THE CASE.

In the case of Walsh *vs.* Whitcomb, (2 Espinasse, pages 565–6,) Lord Kenyon lays down the law in relation to powers of attorney as follows, viz:

"There is a difference in cases of powers of attorney: In general, 'they are revocable from their nature; but there are these exceptions: 'Where a power of attorney is part of a security for money—there it 'is not revocable. Where a power of attorney was given to levy a fine 'as part of a security, it was held not to be revocable. The principle 'is applicable to every case where a power of attorney is necessary to 'effectuate any security; such is not revocable."

Our own Supreme Court have announced the same principle as established law in these United States. In the case of Hunt *vs.* Rousmanier, (8 Wheaton, pages 201–2,) Chief Justice Marshall lays down the law in the following words, viz:

"The general rule is, that a letter of attorney may at any time be 'revoked by the party who makes it, and is revoked by his death. 'But this rule, which results from the nature of the act, has sustained 'some modification. Where a letter of attorney forms a part of a con'tract, and is security for money, or for the performance of any act 'which is deemed valuable, it is generally made irrevocable in terms, 'or, if not so, is deemed irrevocable in law. Although a letter of at-

'torney depends from its nature on the will of the person making it, 'and may in general be revoked at his will; yet, if he binds himself 'for a consideration in terms, or by the nature of his contract, the law 'will not permit him to change it."

The law, as thus laid down, had, prior to our contract with the Western Cherokees, been recognised and acted upon by the Government of the United States.

At page 1,066 of "Attorney Generals' Opinions" there is an opinion of Attorney General B. F. Butler, to the effect that a power of attorney to secure an agent's commission cannot be revoked. His language is as follows, viz:

"In my opinion, the letter of attorney to Mr. Lawrence, executed 'by N. Rogers, surviving executor of the estate, may at any time be 'revoked by him, *except as to the admitted amount of Mr. Lawrence's 'commissions—five per cent.* Your Department, in my opinion, will 'therefore be justified in issuing the certificates on the award to Mr. 'Rogers himself, or to any attorney he may appoint, for 95 per cent. 'thereof, on his due revocation of the former power."

But the principle is much more explicitly laid down by Attorney General Gilpin, in March, 1840, (Churchill's case, pages 1,303–4:)

"Your first inquiry is, whether the provisions of the 9th and 17th 'articles, (which direct that the just debts of the Indians shall be paid 'out of any moneys due them for their improvements and claims, and 'that all claims arising under or provided for by the treaty shall be 'examined and adjudicated by certain commissioners, whose decision 'shall be final,) apply to the case of a person to whom no debt was 'owing at the date of the treaty, but who has acted as an attorney for 'the Indian, for the recovery of his claim, and has had the sum in 'question adjudicated to him as a proper compensation for so acting. 'In reply to this inquiry, I have the honor to say, that I do not con-'sider this to be one of the debts intended to be provided for by the '9th article of the treaty. I am of opinion, however, that if the per-'son presenting the claim was a duly constituted attorney of the In-'dian, with authority to prosecute and recover the claim, and the De-'partment is satisfied that the contract between him and his principal 'is free from fraud, and is a just compensation for services rendered— 'in such case he has an interest in the fund, which the Department 'ought to recognise; and it should not, by paying over the whole 'amount to the Indian, subject him to the probable danger of loss, and 'the certainty of much expense and delay.

"Your second inquiry is, whether the whole scope of the treaty does 'not warrant a payment to the Indians, in person, of such sums as 'may be due to them under it; or whether they must be paid to per-'sons who present powers of attorney from them?

"In reply to this inquiry, I have the honor to state, that the treaty 'clearly recognises payments directly to the Indians, and the Depart-'ment will be fully warranted in so making them. I beg, however, to 'observe, that I consider the remarks I have made in reply to your 'first inquiry as equally applicable to these cases; for, certainly, where 'an attorney has performed an important service, collected the evi-'dence, and been instrumental in securing a claim which might other-

'wise have been lost; and where this has been done under the stipula- 'tion, or with a *bona fide* understanding, that he was to receive the 'amount to which he was entitled directly from the United States, he 'has an interest in the fund, which the principal himself could not re- 'voke, and which the Department is bound to recognise."

It is also a settled practice at common law, that an attorney has a lien upon the judgment of his client. Judge Spencer says, in Johnson's New York Reports, vol. xv., page 405: "It is fully settled, by a long 'series of decisions, that courts of law will take notice of and protect 'the rights of assignees against all persons having either express or 'implied notice of the trust."

These extracts exhibit the law as it existed when our contract with the Western Cherokees was entered into.

1. The highest judicial tribunal of our country had decided that "*Where a letter of attorney forms part of a contract, and is security* 'for money, or *for the performance of any act which is deemed valu- 'able*, it is generally made irrevocable in terms, or, if not so, *is deemed 'irrevocable in law*." * * * That if a party "*binds himself for 'a consideration in terms, or by the nature of his contract, the law 'will not permit him to change it*."

2. This principle had not only been recognised by the Executive branch of our Government, but they had recognised their own obligation to protect the holders of such powers of attorney in the rights acquired by them. In the case of Lawrence, the Government did not consider it "justifiable" to pay his commission over to the original claimant, although a revocation was admitted in every other respect. In the case of Mr. Churchill, such powers of attorney are recognised as creating "*an interest in the fund*." It is even asserted that where an attorney has rendered important services, "under a stipulation, or '(even) with a *bona fide* understanding, that he was to receive the 'amount to which he was entitled *directly from the United States*, he '*has an interest in the fund*, which the principal himself could not re- 'voke, and which THE DEPARTMENT IS BOUND TO RECOGNISE."

Such was the law of the land when we entered into our contract with the Western Cherokees. Let us pause a moment to consider the *reason* of the law. Why will not the Courts permit the revocation of powers of attorney given as security for money, or for services performed? Why did the Executive consider such powers, and even *bona fide* understandings to the same effect, as creating an interest in the fund, which they were bound to recognise? The reason is obvious. *It is to prevent dishonest principals from cheating their agents.* When a principal, having availed himself of the valuable services of an agent, seeks to cheat him out of his compensation, and apply all the proceeds to his own use, by revoking the power of attorney which constitutes the agent's security, an honest Judiciary and an honest Executive have heretofore told him "NO; *your power of attorney gave your 'agent an interest in the fund; the portion which you promised him 'as compensation is no longer yours, but his; as honest administra- 'tors of the law, and dispensers of justice, we are bound to see that it 'goes into his hands, and not into yours*."

I think, sir, yourself and every intelligent lawyer will readily concede, that in this consists the true reason of the law. Bearing in mind the law and its reason, I now beg your attention to

THE FACTS OF THE CASE.

The Western Cherokees, being in great difficulty and distress, solicited our aid in the prosecution of their claim against the United States. Having satisfied ourselves that the claim was just, and that the Delegation which applied to us had as ample authority to make contracts as it was in the power of their people to give, we proposed to serve them for a commission of five per cent. on whatever might be recovered. They had no national or corporate existence *de facto*, no funds nor annuities, nothing whatsoever out of which they could pay their counsel, but the proceeds of the claim which they desired to have prosecuted. Nor had they any credit, or any means of securing their counsel, otherwise than by giving them a lien on those proceeds. This we agreed to take—to serve them for nothing, if nothing was obtained; but, if successful, for five per cent. on the amount recovered, secured by an irrevocable power of attorney, authorizing us to receive it directly from the United States. Not content to rest upon "a *bona fide* understanding," we required a formal written contract, embracing a power of attorney. The following are among its provisions, viz:

"In consideration whereof, the undersigned, John Rogers, John L. 'McCoy, and Ellis F. Phillips, Delegates duly authorized as aforesaid, 'do hereby, on behalf of said Cherokees West, covenant and agree to 'pay, or cause to be paid, the full commission of five per cent. to the 'said A. & J. E. Kendall, upon any sum or sums of money or what-'ever else of value may be allowed and appropriated in full or in part 'satisfaction of said claims, to be paid from time to time, as appropri-'ated or allowed; and the said Delegates do hereby authorize and em-'power the said A. & J. E. Kendall, as agents and attorneys in fact 'for the said Cherokees West, to demand and receive from the treasury 'of the United States, or from the proper office or officer thereof, one-'twentieth part of all sums of money which may be allowed and appro-'priated, or one-twentieth part of any stock, scrip, or any other species 'of funds, securities, or annuities, which may be allowed, to be made 'out and issued in their own names; and if lands or other property, or 'any interest therein, shall be granted in discharge of said claims, or 'any part thereof, to demand and receive from the proper office or offi-'cer a full title to one-twentieth part thereof, it being the true intent 'and meaning of said Delegates that the said A. & J. E. Kendall 'shall receive five per cent., or one-twentieth part, of any and every 'thing of value which may be granted or appropriated on account of 'said claims, to be received directly from the United States without 'any further act or authority by or from the said Cherokees West.

"And the said Delegates do further authorize and empower the said 'A. & J. E. Kendall, as agents and attorneys in fact of the said Chero-'kees West, to sign the names of the said Delegates to any letters and 'memorials to the President, Secretary of War, Senate, House of Rep-'resentatives, or other officer or individual necessary to the prosecution 'and allowance of said claims; and to execute any receipts, acquit-'tances, or other instruments of writing which may be necessary to 'procure the payment or delivery to them, according to the true intent 'and meaning of this instrument, of one-twentieth part of the money, 'property, or evidence of right, title, or claim to any money or property 'which may be appropriated or allowed in satisfaction of said claims 'in full or in part."

For the whole contract, see Senate Ex. Doc. No. 32, 1 Sess. 32 Congress, page 27 to 30.

Now, sir, I submit to your candor, whether it was possible for us by any frame of words more effectually to bring our case within the principle laid down by Lord Kenyon, Chief Justice Marshall, and Attorneys General Butler and Gilpin.

In the language of Lord Kenyon, here is "*a power of attorney necessary to effectuating a security*," which he says "*is not revocable.*"

Here, in the language of Chief Justice Marshall, "*a letter of attorney forms part of a contract*," *and is the only security for the performance of valuable services*—such as he says "*is deemed irrevocable in law.*"

Here there is not a "*bona fide* understanding" merely, but a written "stipulation" that we were to receive the amount to which we might be "entitled *directly from the United States*," which, the Attorney General says, gave us "*an interest in the fund*"—an interest which the Cherokees themselves "*could not revoke*"—an interest which the Government "*is bound to recognise.*"

This contract was based on the same authority as the treaty of 1846—an authority which the United States has not denied, and cannot deny without denying the validity of their own treaty. If there be any desire to examine the authority, a matter not in question, it may be found in Senate Ex. Doc. No. 32, 1 Sess. 32 Congress, page 31.

Through three successive years before the treaty, at the time the treaty was negotiated, and ever since, down to the final payment of the money, as occasion seemed to require, we have applied ourselves to the service of these people. Not only do printed documents abound with arguments prepared by us in the prosecution of their claim, but there are masses of papers of a similar character now on the files of the Indian Office which have never been called out. At length, our enormous labors were crowned with success, and in 1851, eight years after they commenced, the sum of eight hundred eighty-seven thousand four hundred eighty dollars and fifteen cents ($887,480.15) was paid out on account of this claim.

But where is our compensation? Notwithstanding our power of attorney authorizing us to receive it directly from the United States, it has all been distributed among the individual Cherokees. Our irrevocable power of attorney has been virtually revoked; the security which the Law, the Courts, and the Government promised us, has turned out to be wholly illusory; our "interest in the fund" which our principals could not revoke, and which our Government was "bound to recognise" and protect, has been utterly disregarded. Long-established law, which governed our Courts and the Departments of our Government from time immemorial, has been set at naught in our case, for no just end, unless it be just to deprive us of compensation for most laborious and long-continued service in a cause which the Government has finally conceded was a good one. I do not impute dishonest design; but I speak of the effect upon us.

HOW HAS THIS HAPPENED?

The "faith of treaties" is plead as a justification for cheating us! The United States made a treaty with our clients, in which it was stipulated that all the money allowed them for their claim should be distributed *per capita* among the individual Indians. Well, what effect could that treaty have on our compensation? It was secured to us by a power of attorney which the Western Cherokees could not lawfully revoke. Why? Because the law would not allow them to deprive us of our security. If, then, the power of attorney was absolutely irrevocable, it could not be revoked by a treaty between the maker and a third party. A right derived from the Western Cherokees, of which they could not deprive us acting singly, could not lawfully be annihilated by the concurrence of a third party. The treaty, therefore, so far as it purported to take from us our security, a thing which the Western Cherokees could not lawfully do, was null and void; and our interest in the fund remained the same as if no provision had been made for its distribution. Is it not so? If not, the law, as laid down by the highest tribunals and practised upon by our Government, is a delusion and a mockery. The rights of attorneys, with whatever formalities and solemnities secured, are still at the mercy of the maker of the power and the holder of the fund, who may conspire to cheat him out of all compensation and leave him without remedy.

The reason of the law on this point, as we have seen, is to prevent a dishonest principal from cheating his attorney by revoking his power after the service is rendered. It would be dishonest, and therefore is not lawful. The Cherokees could not of themselves do this dishonest thing in our case. Do you not perceive what character the United States assume when they join the Cherokees in an attempt to do it? Can *they* enable the Cherokees to cheat their attorneys in violation of solemn contracts, established law, and moral right, *without incurring any responsibility themselves?*

The fact is, the Cherokee Delegation were blameless in this matter. They opposed the limitation of the fund to pay their debts in the original treaty, lest it should not be sufficient; and when that provision was struck out by the Senate, leaving nothing for that purpose, they never would have concurred in the amendment but for the desperate condition of their affairs, the urgency of the Government, and the advance of $20,000 to pay off their most pressing debts. To show that they did not concur in anything like a revocation of their power of attorney, express or implied, direct or constructive, they made the following endorsement upon our contract, viz:

"The undersigned, Delegates of the Western Cherokees or Old Settlers, being a party to the treaty recently concluded to put an end to 'Cherokee difficulties, do hereby authorize and request the Secretary 'of War to pay the commissions stipulated for in the within contract 'out of any moneys which may be appropriated to pay the debts of the 'Old Settlers, or out of any moneys which may be found due to them 'under the said treaty, it being our intention that this contract shall 'be executed in good faith." (Page 30, Doc. above referred to.)

Here is no revocation or repudiation. Although they had agreed to the treaty, they expressly signified that they did not by that act intend to supersede their contract and revoke their power of attorney; but, on the contrary, intended that it should remain in full force, and that the commissions should be paid directly by the United States.

Now, who is responsible for the dishonest and oppressive effect upon us of the Cherokee treaty of 1846? Is it this Indian delegation who concurred in the treaty upon compulsion, and immediately explained that it was not their intention to impair the security of their attorneys, or deprive them of one iota of their stipulated commissions? Or, is it the United States who forced the treaty upon them, disregarded their explanation and request, and have scattered in the wilderness the funds which ought to have been paid over to us upon every principle of moral honesty, and established law recognised in the administration of our Government?

As if to cut off the possibility of our obtaining our lawful compensation out of the proper fund, Congress put a proviso to the appropriation, in the following words, viz:

"*Provided*, That in no case shall any money hereby appropriated 'be paid to any agent of said Indians, or any other person or persons 'than the Indian or Indians to whom it is due."

This was in effect a declaration that our irrevocable power of attorney should be revoked, not by the party who gave it, but by a third party, who had no interest in the subject; that the principle established by the Supreme Court, and sanctioned by every honest court in Christendom, should be overruled in this case; and that the Executive, in paying out the money, should not regard our "interest in the fund" created by our contract, which, by all previous law, and in administering justice, they were bound to regard!

I know, from the mouth of the Senator who offered the proviso, that he was wholly unaware of its bearings on our case, and had in view the prevention of frauds in cases altogether different. I do not doubt that Senator's sincerity; for I do not believe that he, or any other Senator, would have the inclination or hardihood to offer or vote for a proposition, knowing that its practical effect would be to overthrow established law, rob the laborer of his hire, and set a precedent for repudiators and cheats. Yet, there it is, and the wrong to us is none the less because it was not designed.

Our Government has not done us this great wrong without ample notice.

We were recognised by the Government as the authorized agents of the Western Cherokees from the date of our contract through a period of eight years, during all which it was well known they had no means of payment for services other than the proceeds of the claim we were employed to prosecute.

In February, 1847, we presented the case to Congress in a memorial stating the facts, and prayed that body, in making an appropriation for the Western Cherokees, to provide for the payment of our commissions. This memorial concluded with the declaration that "if 'the United States shall, by their interposition, prevent and refuse 'payment of this contract debt out of the moneys belonging to the Western Cherokees now under their control, they will by such acts and 'refusal become, in the opinion of your memorialists, morally, if not 'legally, bound to pay the debt out of their own Treasury."

In a communication dated June 8, 1848, to the Secretary of War, signed by Colonel Stambaugh and myself, our case was fully stated, a copy of our contract was transmitted, and we prayed for such action as would secure to us our stipulated compensation. See document above referred to, page 35 to 39.

On the 27th of the same month, we again memorialized Congress, and sent with our memorial a copy of our contract. In that paper we held the following language, viz:

"History records many instances in which this Government have 'interposed to compel foreign and *quasi* foreign nations and tribes to 'pay their just debts to American citizens; but this is probably the 'first instance in which a Government has interposed to prevent such a 'payment. The records of the War Department are full of instances 'in which the Government have shown a paternal solicitude to secure 'the payment of debts due from individual Indians to American citizens; but this is a debt of much higher character. It is the debt of 'a *whole tribe, band, or party*—of *that aggregate of people* forming 'one of the three Indian parties to the treaty of 1846.

"Your memorialists have been told that they may collect their debt 'of the individuals of that party. They have no contract with individual Cherokees. The United States did not think it necessary to 'ask the assent of the individuals of that party to the treaty of 1846; 'and to turn over your memorialists to that as a last resort would be 'mockery added to injustice.

"Seeing that the United States have themselves created the only 'obstacle to the payment of this just debt, your memorialists look to 'them for its removal. And if, instead of removing it, they shall dissipate the moneys in their hands in trust for the Western Cherokees, 'regardless of the contract rights now, as well as heretofore, made 'known, your memorialists will have a right to consider the United 'States their debtor, and never cease to ask for payment until it shall 'be obtained. No claim for French or Mexican spoliations can be 'half so strong; for in this case the Government *itself* will have been 'the only wrongdoer, being *itself* the author of the provisions in the 'treaty under cover of which the wrong will have been done, and having '*itself, after notice*, dissipated the funds upon which the debt is justly 'chargeable. Where else *can* your memorialists look for justice, inasmuch as the tribe, or body of men, with whom they contracted, is 'alleged by the United States to have been annihilated by the treaty, 'and all its property will have been distributed among its members.

"Your memorialists, therefore, most respectfully pray that provision 'be made for the payment of the commission justly due to them out of 'the moneys which have been or may be appropriated for the benefit of 'the Western Cherokees under the treaty of 1846, in pursuance of the 'terms of their contract."

As early as June, 1848, therefore, both the Executive and Congress had full notice of this claim, and were in possession of copies of the contract embracing the irrevocable power of attorney on which it was based.

On the 18th January, 1849, the Senate adopted a resolution calling on the Secretary of War for information in relation to claims against the Cherokees, and particularly the Old Settlers or Western Cherokees. On the 9th February, 1849, the Secretary responded to this call, transmitting among other things a copy of our contract, and the authority on which it was based, together with several recognitions of the contract after the treaty was ratified, voluminous arguments in favor of the claims of the Western Cherokees, and the letter of Colonel Stambaugh and myself asking for some provision to secure payment of our commissions according to contract. This report constitutes Senate Executive Document No. 28, Second Session, Thirtieth Congress. Permit me to call your attention to it, particularly to our contract marked B, on pages 6, 7, 8, 9, to its special recognition on page 9, to its general recognition on pages 11, 14, and 25, and to the letter of Colonel Stambaugh and myself on pages 15 to 20.

In this document, page 4, the Commissioner of Indian Affairs, Hon. W. Medill, says: "The files of the Department attest the assiduity 'and ability with which Messrs. Stambaugh and Kendall attended to 'the duty intrusted to them; and I think it highly probable that the ''Western Cherokees,' or 'Old Settlers,' are greatly indebted for the 'stipulations made for their benefit in the treaty of 1846 to the re'searches and persevering efforts of their counsel. The evidence on 'which I have based my opinion is *my own knowledge of the personal 'exertions of the counsel named, and that shown in the accompanying 'papers.*" He then refers to the papers, which in fact do not embrace a third part of those prepared by us in this case, as I am prepared to show.

This document brought the whole subject before Congress in the most formal manner; but nothing was done for our relief.

At the next meeting of Congress, the new Commissioner of Indian Affairs, Orlando Brown, Esq., in his annual report, called the attention of Congress to the subject in the following words, viz:

"A considerable amount will be due to that portion of the Chero'kees known as the Old (or original) Settlers, west of the Mississippi, 'who, as a separate and distinct community, have incurred liabilities 'of various kinds; and among others for valuable and efficient services 'rendered them in prosecuting their claims against the Government, 'and which, it is well known, were greatly instrumental in effecting the 'recognition of those claims, and the large allowances in consideration 'of them. In the treaty as negotiated, a provision was inserted setting 'apart a portion of the sum to be awarded them to enable them to meet 'such liabilities, but for some cause not known it was struck out by the 'Senate; so that the whole amount is now liable, according to the 'naked terms of the treaty as it now stands, to a per capita distribu'tion. Unless some change in this particular be in some way author'ized, the just and honorable intentions of the Indians themselves will 'be defeated, and great injustice done to their creditors—which should 'by all means be avoided."

At the same session we again memorialized Congress; and on the 10th August, 1850, Mr. Sebastian, from the Committee on Indian Affairs in the Senate, made a favorable report. See Senate Reports No. 180, First Session, Thirty-First Congress.

This report recognised every principle on which we base our claim, viz:

1. That our contract was valid.
2. That the lien it gave us on the funds of the Western Cherokees was irrevocable.
3. That the services had been faithfully performed.
4. That the treaty of 1846 did not impair our lien.
5. That, in default of that fund, the debt survived against the United States.

The following is the reasoning of the Committee, viz:

"When these engagements were entered into, the Western Cherokees were a distinct party, forming, in fact, a separate political body, and directing their separate interests through the action of a 'national council.' As such they were recognised, through their delegations and their agents, from 1842 until and at the making of the treaty of 1846, in which the United States regarded them as having distinct interests and competent to release their separate claim to the country east, and agree to an indemnity for it. This same authority had created this debt against the 'Western Cherokees,' and secured it by an equitable lien on the funds to be paid them under that treaty, of which the United States were fully cognizant. At this time it was a debt against the 'Western Cherokees,' for which any national fund of theirs would be liable generally, but that under the treaty *specifically*. By that treaty, provision was made for setting apart the sum of $50,000 to discharge their national debts; but this provision was stricken out by the Senate, the effect of which was to appropriate the whole of their money due under that treaty to a *per capita* distribution. Thus the *treaty fund was gone*. The clause of the treaty which merged all the different parties in one common nation, and under one government, destroyed their separate political existence, 'except for the purpose of executing the treaty.' Thus every national fund was gone, and the nation extinguished. Against whom did the debt survive? Not against the individual Cherokees, for they were not parties to it. Not against the nation, for that was extinct. Not against the whole nation of Cherokees, for the union was political, and had no reference to the separate debts of its factions; but the debt survived, and against the fund pledged for its payment, or, in default of that, against the United States. The Cherokees could not by the treaty release their obligation, nor could the United States, neither debtor nor creditor, release it. But they could by the treaty enter into an obligation *inconsistent with its payment*, and thus become responsible for it themselves. Other means of payment being exhausted, either the United States are liable, if the treaty has *released the fund*, or the fund is liable, if the treaty has not destroyed the lien. That there was a specification and appropriation of so much of that fund as was necessary to pay the debt, cannot, we think, be questioned. It was created by an authority competent to do it. The 'pledge was irrevocable. It was not a mere agency to receive, but an 'equitable transfer of so much of the fund. It was a security for pay-'ment; and if the United States has discharged it, they are liable for 'the debt."

The Committee, however, being of opinion that the fund was still chargeable with our commissions, recommended "that in the proper 'appropriation bill a provision should be adopted setting apart a cer-'tain amount of the sum due the Western Cherokees for satisfaction of 'these claims."

So far from complying with this recommendation, however, the Senate adopted the proviso already quoted, *prohibiting* the payment of any portion of the fund to agents!

Finally, the moneys appropriated were placed in the hands of the disbursing agent, and we took counsel and advised with him in relation to preventing by injunction the distribution of our portion of them among the individual Indians. The agent informed us that he would not obey such an injunction if obtained, and we were advised that it was very doubtful whether we could avail ourselves of such a remedy. For the fourth time we laid our case before Congress, which was then in session. The following was a portion of our representation and prayer, viz:

"It is not the individual Indian, but the whole body, that is the 'debtor of your memorialists; and they could have little hope that the 'individuals, when thus virtually told by Congress that they were not 'bound, would bind themselves, when, instead of gaining anything by 'it, they would lose a portion of the glittering temptation placed within 'their reach. Nor could they shut their eyes to the facts that there 'would be many persons around the Indian Agency who would dissuade 'the individual Indians from paying this debt, from interested or vin-'dictive considerations.

"Your memorialists hoped that another resource was left to them in 'the Judiciary of their country, by whose instrumentality they might 'be able to stop the funds in the hands of the disbursing agent of the 'Government; but they are advised that the power of the Judiciary to 'grant them redress is extremely questionable; and they have been 'assured by the agent who now has the funds in his hands, that he will 'not regard any such Judicial mandate.

"Under these circumstances, they again look to your Honorable 'Bodies for relief. It will be some months before these moneys can 'be paid out to the Indians—ample time to give effect to any act of 'legislation adopted at the present session.

"Your memorialists ask for nothing which they have not a right to 'claim and receive according to the principles of law and equity which 'govern courts of justice in civilized and Christian nations; and they 'now pray for such legislation as will secure the payment of the debt 'out of the funds appropriated for the benefit of the 'Western Chero-'kees,' or out of the Treasury of the United States; but they will be 'perfectly content with a resolution or act enabling them to enjoin the 'payment of the moneys in the hands of the disbursing officer until 'their claims can be judicially investigated and decided."

But Congress were wholly deaf to our prayer.

Again we turned to the Executive, and in a letter dated March 14, 1851, "*protested against the payment to the Western Cherokees of the ' one-twentieth part of those moneys, being the interest assigned to us ' for services prior to the ratification of the treaty.*" We said, "The ' question we now wish to submit is, whether the United States, with ' everybody's eyes open as to the wrong, (not to use a harsher word,) ' are bound to proceed through the Indian Office to the consummation ' of that wrong, by paying to the Cherokees, individually, moneys which ' were assigned away by competent authority, and for a valuable con- ' sideration, long before the treaty was formed?" We endeavored to satisfy him that the payment of our moneys to the Cherokees would be the consummation of a palpable fraud upon us; that neither the treaty nor act of Congress ought to be construed so as to require or justify a fraud; and we concluded with the following prayer, viz:

"We therefore respectfully ask at your hands an order to Colonel ' Drennen, who now has charge of the fund, to pay us the twentieth ' part thereof without further trouble, including interest thereon as al- ' lowed by Congress. If, in consequence of steps already taken, or any ' other cause, the Department hesitates to give such an order, then we ' most respectfully request that the opinion of the Attorney General ' may be taken upon the points involved, not doubting that his talents ' and legal skill will enable him to point out some line of proceeding ' consistent at the same time with the rights of the citizen and the obli- ' gations of the Government." For the whole letter, see Senate Ex. Doc. No. 32, 1 Sess. 32 Congress, pages 20 to 23.

But no order was given, nor was the opinion of the Attorney General asked for.

The Secretary of the Interior and the Commissioner of Indian Affairs were perfectly satisfied of the justice of our claim; but considering themselves precluded from paying it by the proviso of Congress, they proposed to aid us in collecting it of the Western Cherokees by sending out an agent for that purpose. Evidence of this suggestion is found in my letter of the 19th June, 1851, to be found in the Document last above named, pages 71 to 74.

On page 74 may be found a letter from me to the Secretary of the Interior, dated July 1, 1851, containing the following passage, viz:

"The suggestion and request I have to make is, that Colonel Dren- ' nen be instructed not only to obey an injunction which may be ob- ' tained in our case and that of Colonel Stambaugh, but that, in case ' of difficulty with the Indians, he will give time to apply for and ob- ' tain one before making payment. I think that such instructions, ' coupled with a strong expression of opinion from your Department ' that these debts ought to be paid, would prevent all trouble."

No answer was received.

Having learnt that a spirit of repudiation had sprung up in the Cherokee country, putting an end to all hope of a voluntary payment of our claims by the general assent of the Western Cherokees, I addressed another letter to the Secretary of the Interior, dated August 17th, 1851, concluding as follows, viz:

"I appeal to you, sir, to avert from our Government and country ' for the present, and enable Congress to avert forever, the stigma 'which cannot but attach to the consummation of such an outrage. On 'behalf of A. & J. E. Kendall and Colonel S. C. Stambaugh, whose 'aggregate claims amount to ten per cent. on the appropriations for the 'benefit of the Western Cherokees or Old Settlers, I request and en- 'treat an official order to Colonel Drennen, directing him to withhold 'that amount to await the further action of Congress. Surely, the 'nature of the case, as now understood, will justify if it do not require 'this exercise of power on your part.

"And in view of the wrong now about to be consummated, unless 'prevented by your prompt interposition, it will not be deemed amiss 'in me most respectfully to *repeat the protest heretofore made against 'being sent to the Cherokee country to collect moneys which by con- 'tract are payable at Washington, and again give notice that we, 'the counsel of the Western Cherokees, look to our Government 'for the payment of our claims and of all expenses, losses, and dama- 'ges which have been or may be occasioned to us by its own wrong in 'this behalf.*"

To this letter I received no answer.

Although the Secretary of the Interior and the Commissioner of Indian Affairs recognised the justice of our claim, they did not think themselves authorized, after the action of Congress, to do more than give us the benefit of their opinion, and advise the Indians to make payment. To that end, the Secretary of the Interior wrote the following letter to the Commissioner of Indian Affairs, viz:

"I have examined the instructions you propose to give to Mr. Dren- 'nen in regard to the payments to be made to the Cherokees, and cor- 'dially approve them. You will please add to them that I have care- 'fully examined the claims of Messrs. Thompson, Harris, and Ken- 'dalls, against the Indians, for professional services, and, from the evi- 'dence before me, I am satisfied that they are just and reasonable, 'and should be paid. If I had possessed the legal authority, I should 'have felt no hesitation in ordering their payment; but, as it is at 'least questionable whether I had the power to do so, I determined to 'refrain from such an interference. I regretted this the less, however, 'because I am persuaded the Indians will be disposed to fulfil their 'obligations in good faith when they are properly explained by Colonel 'Drennen."

The instructions alluded to recommended the raising of a committee by the Indians, to examine the claims against them, and the payment of such as they found to be just.

Protesting against the course pursued, and declaring that we still held the United States responsible for our claim, and for all losses and damages that might ensue from thus compelling us to seek justice from the individual Cherokees, who were not our debtors, John E. Kendall visited the Cherokee country in the hope that the Indians, influenced by Colonel Drennen and the decided opinion of the Government, would permit the payment of our claim. The committee was appointed; but so high was the excitement against paying the large amount of just debts due from the Western Cherokees, that, for a time, it was doubted whether they would venture to act at all. At length, however, they met, allowed the whole of Colonel Stambaugh's claim, and threw ours out altogether, on the pretext that the stipulated service had not been rendered! We seem to see the venerable chief, John Rogers, start in his grave at an allegation from his survivors so atrociously false! The only excuse for them is, that *they dared not allow all the claims they knew to be just, through fears of assassination.*

After incurring heavy expenses, and suffering much from sickness, my nephew returned to Washington. And, now, there are those who would construe this effort, *made under protest*, as a relinquishment of our claim on the Government!

The public documents are so full of testimony that we performed the service zealously, perseveringly, and successfully, that it seems a work of supererogation to produce further evidence. Yet, after learning on what pretext the Cherokee committee had refused to recognise our claim, we addressed every gentleman then living, who, as a public officer, had cognizance of this Cherokee business, (except Commissioners Medill and Brown, whose testimony to our fidelity we had in their official reports,) and we annex their answers. In contradiction of the Indian committee, therefore, we have the evidence of the following gentlemen, viz:

Hon. J. M. Porter, late Secretary of War.
Hon. Wm. Wilkins, " "
Hon. W. L. Marcy, " "
Hon. A. H. H. Stuart, Secretary of the Interior.
Hon. T. Hartley Crawford, late Commissioner of Indian Affairs.
Hon. W. Medill, " "
Hon. Orlando Brown, " "
Hon. Luke Lea, present Commissioner of Indian Affairs.
Charles E. Mix, Esq., Acting Commissioner of Indian Affairs.
Hon. Edmund Burke, one of the commissioners who negotiated the treaty of 1846.
Hon. Albion K. Parris, the other surviving commissioner, who also, as Comptroller of the Treasury, settled the Cherokee accounts.

And to this overwhelming testimony we are prepared to add a heavy mass of papers prepared by us in this case, which have never found their way into the printed documents of Congress.

MR. BADGER'S SPEECH.

With the law and the facts of the case before us, let us now examine briefly the positions assumed by you in opposition to our claim.

The following extract from your speech, as reported in the *Union* of the 17th of August last, embraces the substance of your argument, viz:

" My friend has referred to this contract. He says, what does it 'signify what the treaty contains—here is the contract? I ask him, 'in turn, what does it signify what the contract says? The United 'States have no part in that contract. That is an agreement between 'the Indians and their agents for prosecuting this claim. Does that 'affect this Government, and estop us from paying the money to the 'Indians, and control our action in any way? Certainly not. The 'Government cannot be estopped in any case; that is a settled princi- 'ple. But no individual could be estopped in this way. Again: the 'truth is, that according to the rule adopted in the Executive Depart-

'ment, these persons could have had no claim upon this money, even 'if it had been paid without this amendment. What is the contract? 'These persons, on behalf of the Cherokees West, 'covenant and agree 'to pay, or cause to be paid, the full commission of five per cent.' 'That authorizes them to receive the commission of five per cent., or 'one-twentieth part. And it goes on to say that it 'shall be received 'directly from the United States,' &c. Now, the rule in the Depart-'ment is this: they do not undertake to enforce contracts to pay; they 'have never assumed any such jurisdiction. What they have done is 'this, and that is sanctioned by the usage of the Department, and 'nothing more: Where there is an actual assignment, in terms, trans-'ferring to the agent, in consideration of services rendered, or to be 'rendered, a certain proportion of the claims, they have considered him 'as an equitable owner of that portion of the claim, and have paid it 'to him—not in virtue of a contract for services, but as the assignee 'of that portion. And where there is an assignment, the Department 'have considered that assignment as passing property, and are in the 'habit of enforcing it. But the Department have never undertaken to 'enforce contracts with agents; and as long as the claim rests merely 'upon the contract, they do not touch it. Where there is an assign-'ment of ten per cent., they have assumed that the agent had an inter-'est in one-tenth of the claim, and have paid it to him, and then paid 'the other nine-tenths to the principal. But if the principal, instead 'of making an assignment, enters into a contract to pay a compensa-'tion—no matter what it is—the Department have never assumed 'jurisdiction over it.

"It seems to me, therefore, that this claim is stripped of every ten-'able ground. Even if the parties had appeared at the Department, 'and the contract had been denied by the Indians, and they had re-'fused their assent and consent to the contract, the Department would 'have had no jurisdiction over this matter, because it is not an actual 'assignment to these agents. In the first place, this Government had 'a right to pay the money directly to the principal, and the agents 'cannot complain that we did so pay it. In the next place, the agents 'had no interest upon the principal which could be enforced at the 'Department, and therefore the payment of the principal has caused 'them no loss; and therefore they can bring no claim against the Gov-'ernment. It seems to me, therefore, that this claim is without 'foundation."

Upon this I most respectfully submit the following remarks, viz:

1. I cannot think you had read and fully considered the character of our contract. It is not, as you seem to suppose, a naked contract by which the Western Cherokees "covenant and agree to pay, or cause to be paid, the full commission of five per cent.," which "shall be received directly from the United States," as you seem to suppose; but it goes further, and *embraces a power of attorney*. It says, "and the 'said delegates do hereby authorize and empower the said A. & J. E. 'Kendall, *as agents and attorney in fact for the said Cherokees West*, '*to demand and receive from the Treasury of the United States, or* '*from the proper office or officer thereof, one-twentieth part of all the* '*sums of money which may be allowed and appropriated*," &c., "*it*

'*being the true intent and meaning of said delegates, that the said A. & J. E. Kendall shall receive five per cent., or one-twentieth part of any and every thing of value which may be granted or appropriated on account of said claims, to be received directly from the United States, without any further act or authority by or from the said Cherokees West.*"

In short, we had "*a letter of attorney coupled with a contract*" as our security in the arduous duty we undertook. Is it not so? We appeal to you to say whether it was possible for us, by any form of words, to bring ourselves more effectually within the protection of the law as laid down by Chief Justice Marshall.

2. We were told by the Attorney General, whose opinions regulated the practice of the Departments, that "a stipulation," or "a *bona fide* understanding," that we were to receive our commissions directly from the United States, would give us "*an interest in the fund,*" which the Western Cherokees "could not revoke, and which *the Department was bound to recognise.*"

Our contract was not only "a *bona fide* understanding" and "a stipulation," but it was more—it gave us an express and irrevocable power of attorney. By the law, as laid down and practised upon by the Government itself, our contract gave us "an interest in the fund," which it "was bound to recognise." And shall the law as laid down then be now changed, not to promote justice, but to cover injustice!

3. You admit that, where there is an assignment, the Government is bound to regard it, and does regard it. I am not lawyer enough to perceive the difference in law or common sense between an interest created by the word "assign" and one created by other words which equally put the interest embraced so completely beyond the reach of the party using them as to require "no further act or authority by or from them" to perfect the transfer. If an irrevocable power of attorney is not, so far as legal right is concerned, tantamount to an assignment—if not in law an actual assignment—it is a mockery. Your view of the matter arises from a misconception of our power of attorney. You say:

"We paid this money according to the terms of the treaty. By our own act we required that it should be paid *per capita*, and we so paid it. And now we are gravely told that if we had allowed the money to go into the hands of the agent, *he would have deducted his compensation*, and everything would have been perfectly straight. But inasmuch as we paid the money to the principal, and the principal refuses to pay the agent, we are bound to make it good to him. The whole question resolves itself into this: If A is agent of B in reference to a claim against C, does that absolve the debtor C from paying the debt to the principal B? Certainly not."

If you will examine our power of attorney, you will perceive that it never gave us the authority to receive the *whole* of this money with a view to the deduction of our compensation; but it only authorized us to receive the portion set apart as our compensation. Our complaint is, not that the United States paid directly to the Cherokees the portion belonging to them, but that they did not, after full notice, pay to us the portion belonging to us.

To make the case you put parallel, some new features must be introduced into it. A, being the agent of B for the collection of a claim upon C, takes from B, as security for his compensation, an irrevocable power of attorney authorizing him to receive it of C, *of which A gives C notice.* Does not that absolve the debtor C from paying that portion of the debt to the principal B? Certainly it does. It goes further—it *binds him not to pay it to B;* and if he does so, the law will compel him to pay it over again to A. Otherwise, what security is there in an irrevocable power of attorney? If C, *after notice*, can lawfully pay the amount of A's compensation to B, the agent A, by collusion between B and C, may be cheated out of his compensation, however irrevocable in terms may be his power of attorney. I think Chief Justice Marshall would have decided that the object of the law could not be thus defeated.

Now, this is precisely our case. The Western Cherokees (B) come to the Messrs. Kendalls, (A,) and employ us to prosecute a claim against the United States, (C,) and, by way of security for our compensation, give us an irrevocable power of attorney authorizing us to receive our commissions directly from the United States; and *of the existence of this power the Messrs. Kendalls (A) give ample notice to the United States, (C.)* Now, can the United States, *after such notice*, lawfully pay those commissions over to the Western Cherokees, (B?) If they can, Lord Kenyon, Chief Justice Marshall, Attorney General Gilpin and the Government of that day, were wholly mistaken in the law.

And here we beg you to consider as a lawyer whether *an interest created by an irrevocable power of attorney, with notice, given for a consideration*, is not in law precisely equivalent to *an interest created by an assignment, with notice, executed for a consideration?* We beg of you also to inquire whether interests created by irrevocable powers of attorney given for a consideration, or by "*bona fide* understandings" and "stipulations" in the nature of such powers, have not in fact been considered by the Department as assigned interests, so far at least as to merit and receive its protection? We *know* that such interests were protected when we made our contract with the Western Cherokees, and we believe no case can be found prior to ours on the records of the Government in which such interests have been disregarded. In short, we look upon our interest as in all essential features precisely such an one as you say it has been the practice of the Department to protect, and we are sure that on further investigation you will come to the same conclusion.

4. But you say "we (meaning the Government) certainly have the right of paying the money to the persons to whom we owe it, if we please." You also say "the Government cannot be estopped in any case."

Now, we supposed our Government was a Government of laws. We supposed that, when the Supreme Court lays down a principle as law, the Government is bound to regard it as law. We supposed that, when the Attorney General said the Government was bound by certain peculiar transactions between its creditors and their agents, it was really bound. We supposed that, when a principle was announced as law, and practised upon as law by the Government itself, it was bound by that law. But if the officials constituting our Government cannot be estopped by any law, we have entirely misconceived the character of the institutions under which we live. If your position as broadly laid down be correct, it is a lawless despotism, instead of being a Government of laws. Our experience in this case, we confess, tends to establish your position.

You—I mean the Government—by professing to be governed by certain laws, led us to undertake a most laborious duty upon a security which those laws assured us was amply sufficient—being such as our principals could not retract, and such as you told us you were bound to recognise.

Upon your faith, we spent months and years of toilsome research and labor in convincing you that you had grievously wronged our unhappy clients.

As if to punish us for convincing you of the wrongs you have committed, you do not indeed conspire with our clients to cheat us; but you *force upon them* a treaty provision which, you say, cuts off our entire compensation. You wrong us by making such a treaty, and then plead your own wrong in justification of the results it produces.

Lest an honest Executive should consider of no effect so much of the treaty as purports to nullify our power of attorney, and rob us of our interest in the fund, you follow up the blow with a proviso forbidding the payment to us of one dollar of the money!

In vain the Western Cherokee Delegation tell you they did not intend to nullify or impair their power of attorney.

In vain we call your attention to the law which declared it could not be nullified.

In vain we present you with your own admission that you were bound to regard the interest which it created, and with your own practice holding such interest sacred.

In vain we call your attention to the report of one of your own committees, telling you that you will be bound to pay this money yourself if you pay it out to the Indians.

Notice upon notice, memorial upon memorial, letter upon letter, are wholly disregarded, and our money is thrown broadcast into the Western wilderness.

Though our contract and your treaty are made by the same Delegation, and upon precisely the same authority, you hold every Western Cherokee bound by your treaty, while you allow every Western Cherokee to repudiate our contract.

You send us to the Cherokee country to collect our money of the individual Indians, and because we go, though under formal protest, hoping to fare better at the hands of savages than at those of our own Government, you now seem inclined to construe that compulsory act as giving up our recourse upon you!

An expensive and hazardous effort to collect from them a debt due from you, though done under protest, is said by some to relieve you from responsibility!

We are American citizens, entitled to the protection of our Government in our lawful transactions with foreigners. The Western Cherokees were so far foreign that no law of the United States enforcing contracts could reach them.

You send Ministers to civilized nations to make reclamations, when foreign Governments seize and sequestrate the property of your merchants. You threaten reprisals and war if they do not make reparation. You send your armed ships to the other side of the globe to punish with fire and sword the lawless barbarians who plunder your merchant ships and refuse to restore the plunder. Yet, here at home, you not only unite with a half-civilized people to prevent the payment by them of a defined and liquidated debt to your citizens, but you are yourself the instigator of the fraud, and the instrument—the voluntary instrument—of its consummation.

If you had held the moneys of France in your treasury sufficient to pay the indemnities to our merchants, would you have hesitated, instead of threatening war, to have applied them to that purpose? If you had held the moneys of Mexico sufficient to pay all the claims of our citizens upon her, would you have sent your army and navy to seize upon her cities and conquer her provinces? In both of these cases, would you not, instead of hostile measures, have paid over the money to your citizens, even without the authority or consent of Mexico and France? And if, instead of doing so, you had paid it over to those Governments, and, as your apology, told your citizens, their creditors, that you had "the right of paying the money to the persons to whom you owed it," and that "the Government could not be estopped," would you not have been denounced, not only through the length and breadth of this land, but throughout the civilized world, as faithless to your trust, and derelict in the highest duties of a Government to its citizens?

You held the moneys of the Western Cherokees, who, in relation to pecuniary transactions with your citizens, were foreign. You were informed that your citizens held a liquidated and acknowledged claim upon them. It would seem this was enough to induce a paternal Government, tenacious of the rights of its citizens, and proudly displaying its flag in every sea, to evince its determination to defend them, at once to pay the debt out of the debtor's money. How much higher was the obligation when we held an *express* and *irrevocable lien* upon the fund, which, by the rules heretofore regulating your action, you were bound to recognise! But, instead of recognising the obligation and discharging the debt out of the Western Cherokee fund, you not only dissipate that fund, but by your treaty *annihilate our original debtor!* In other cases, if you refuse protection to your citizens, the foreign Government which has wronged them remains, to whose justice and magnanimity they may appeal for redress. But in this case, you not only refuse to secure our debt when you can, but you exterminate our debtor. Refusing to recognise his irrevocable power of attorney, you put him to death, and, handing our money over to his insolvent heirs, tell us to *get it if we can!*

We repress the indignant feelings which rise up when we reflect how we have been treated in this matter. But, conscious of no offence against our Government or fellow-citizens which can justify outlawry and confiscation, we attribute this treatment to the mistakes and inattention of those whose duty it was to protect our rights, rather than any design to do us injustice.

In conclusion, permit us to ask you to decide, in all candor, upon the following propositions, viz:

Ought not our commissions to have been paid by somebody?

Whose fault was it that they were not paid out of the Western Cherokee fund?

If you think we ought to have been paid, and that it was the fault of the Government that we were not paid out of the proper fund, then your public and private character is a guarantee to us, that hereafter you will be found among those who insist that the Government which has done the wrong, shall repair the injury.

With unfeigned respect,

Your obedient servant,

AMOS KENDALL.

P. S. For the previous practice of our Government in the payment of attorneys' and agents' fees, see the letter of Hon. L. Lea, of 8th April, 1852, on page 27.

APPENDIX.

DEPARTMENT OF THE INTERIOR, *July* 18, 1851.

SIR: I have examined the instructions which you propose to give to Mr. Drennen in regard to the payments to be made to the Cherokees, and cordially approve them. You will please add to them that I have carefully examined the claims of Messrs. Thompson, Harris, and Kendalls, against the Indians, for professional services; and, from the evidence before me, I am satisfied that they are just and reasonable, and should be paid. If I had possessed the legal authority, I should have felt no hesitation in ordering their payment; but as it was at least questionable whether I had the power to do so, I determined to refrain from such an interference. I regretted this the less, however, because I am persuaded the Indians will be disposed to fulfil their obligations in good faith, when they are properly explained by Mr. Drennen.

Very respectfully, your obedient servant,

ALEX. H. H. STUART, *Secretary.*

CHARLES E. MIX, Esq.,
Acting Commissioner of Indian Affairs.

GADSBY'S HOTEL, WASHINGTON, *January* 20, 1852.

DEAR SIR: Your letter of the 19th instant has been received. I was surprised to learn from it, as I did, that your claim against the Western Cherokee Indians, for services rendered them as agent and counsel in advocating their claims against the Government of the United States before the Board of Commissioners appointed to negotiate the Treaty of 1846, had been rejected by a committee of Indians, on the ground that you had been unfaithful to their interests; while the claim of Colonel Stambaugh, your colleague, for similar services, had been allowed and paid.

Having had ample opportunity, as one of the Commissioners who negotiated the Treaty, to observe your conduct on that occasion, as well as that of all others who appeared as agents or counsel before the commissioners, I am confident I can say, without reflecting on any individual concerned, that no one was more faithful, untiring, and zealous in the advocacy of the cause of his clients, than you were in behalf of the interests of yours. It was my opinion (and I think I can say the same for my surviving colleague on that board, Judge Parris) that you urged the cause of your clients, not only with all necessary zeal and perseverance, but with a degree of skill and ability surpassed by no other counsel who appeared, (before the board.) Certainly, on that occasion, you did nothing which could tend to the injury of the interests of your clients, and omitted nothing which would tend to promote them. And I never knew you on any other occasion to do anything tending to prejudice, nor omit to do anything tending to promote, the interests of that portion of the Cherokee Indians whom you, in connection with Colonel Stambaugh, represented before the Government of the United States.

We made provision in the Treaty for the payment in part of your claim. That provision was stricken out by the Senate. It is certainly hard that you, who contributed so much to the settlement of the unhappy controversies and murderous feuds then existing among the different factions of the Cherokee Indians, should be deprived of all compensation for the very able services which you rendered, not only to your clients, but to the Government and to humanity, on that occasion. In my opinion, your services were quite as valuable, and contributed as much to the success of your clients, on the occasion referred to, as those of Colonel Stambaugh.

I am, with great respect, your obedient servant,

EDMUND BURKE.

Hon. Amos Kendall.

Easton, Pennsylvania, *January* 22, 1852.

Dear Sir: I have a very perfect recollection that, when I had the honor to fill the Department of War—from early in March, 1843, until about the close of January, 1844—the claim of the Western Cherokees was before the Department. I can also bear testimony to the zeal, fidelity, and ability, with which you, as their advocate, urged and pressed those claims upon the Government whilst the subject was before me; and I was much indebted to your indefatigable industry and untiring zeal for the knowledge of the details, as well as the principles of the claim, which I obtained. If they have since obtained a recognition and allowance of their claim against the Government, they are greatly indebted to your exertions on their behalf for it.

It is not possible for me now, without recurrence to documents, to go into details; but the impression is very strong on my mind of how assiduous you were in urging the claim, clearing up real or supposed difficulties, and casting much light upon it.

I am, very truly, yours,

J. M. PORTER.

Hon. Amos Kendall, *Washington City*.

Albany, *January* 23, 1852.

Dear Sir: In reply to your letter of the 19th instant, I state that I well recollect you presented to me, when Secretary of War, several elaborate communications in relation to the Cherokee difficulties, and the claims which were made by the Cherokees, or some one of the parties among them, upon the United States. These difficulties were settled by a Commission, on which were Mr. Edmund Burke and Judge Parris. It was a very complicated matter, and I thought at the time that you did much to bring it about. Besides the communications you made to the Department, which showed that you must have spent much time and bestowed much labor on the subject, you had several interviews with me, in which you strongly pressed the claims of one party of that divided nation. Through the whole of that controversy I thought you were active, persevering, and devoted to the interest of the section of the nation whose cause you had espoused. So far as it appeared to me, you did more than any other person to bring about the adjustment which was made, and by which a large claim was established against the United States.

Yours, truly,

W. L. MARCY.

Hon. A. Kendall, Esq.

Washington, *January* 24, 1852.

My Dear Sir: I received your communication of 19th inst., in relation to the non-payment of a proper remuneration to you by the Western Cherokees, for services rendered in prosecution of their claim, requesting an answer from me to certain interrogatories propounded.

I have delayed a reply, that I might reflect on the subject, with a view to recalling to my mind the circumstances to which you refer. You appeared at the Indian Office personally and by written communications and arguments on the part of the Western Cherokees, (John Rogers and others,) and advocated their claim with ability and zeal. Infidelity to their interests, you say, is the pretext for refusing a proper compensation to you. This, I think, does you the grossest injustice in reference to both character and compensation, and so I am sure the records of the office will show it to be.

I cannot answer the interrogatories put, without reference to the papers on file in the Indian Office. I have taxed my memory in vain as to particulars—of which I have, in the many years that have passed, now more than six, since I left the Department, lost all reliable trace; and I am engaged daily in Court from 10 A. M. to 4 and 5 o'clock P. M.

If you think it important to you, I will, at your request, as soon as my Court is over, go to the Indian Office and examine the papers on file; which, however, will only enable me to answer as they may show the facts—and, in my judgment, you will find in those papers better evidence than my testimony would furnish.

With respect and regard, your obedient servant,

T. HARTLEY CRAWFORD.

Hon. Amos Kendall, *Washington, D. C.*

Portland, Maine, *January* 26, 1852.

Sir: I was indeed much surprised to learn, from your letter of the 19th inst., that the Western Cherokees, for whom you acted as agent in negotiating the Treaty of 1846, have refused you all compensation for your services, upon the pretext that you were not faithful to their interests.

Having been one of the Commissioners on the part of the United States, I had as good opportunity as any one to know the measures taken and the grounds urged by the different branches of the Cherokee nation in support of their respective claims.

As agent for the "Old Settlers, or Western Cherokees," you in the outset took the ground that they were the owners of the territory ceded by the Treaty of 1828, and had the exclusive title thereto—which ground you supported by an able written argument, manifestly the result of much labor and research. I have the more distinct recollection of what relates to this claim of the Western Cherokees, from the fact that your argument made a deep impression upon the Commissioners, and it was not until after much deliberation that we came to the conclusion set forth in the fourth article of the Treaty. This mode of avoiding the exclusive claim set up by the Western Cherokees was first suggested by myself, and was acquiesced in by the other members of the Commission on the part of the United States, as the only way by which an adjustment could be made that would be ratified by all parties.

I well recollect your unwillingness to accede to the proposition, and your strenuous efforts to produce a different result, that would secure to the Western Cherokees the whole territory ceded by the Treaty of 1828.

It was difficult to avoid the claim. To admit it, would have prevented any adjustment of the serious difficulties existing between the different portions of the Cherokee nation.

In coming to a decision upon this most perplexing branch of the case, we were induced by a consideration of the merits of the Western Cherokees, set forth in your argument, to make more liberal provisions for them than for either of the other branches of the Cherokee nation.

I know that you attended to the interests of those people ably and faithfully, and I am not aware that you omitted anything that their interests required to be done, or that any one did more than you did in their behalf. With great respect, ALBION K. PARRIS.

Hon. Amos Kendall.

Homewood, *January* 30, 1852.

My Dear Sir: There has been some delay in the arrival of our mails, and your letter of the 19th inst. has only just now been put into my hands.

In reference to your action and interference in behalf of and advocating the claim of the Western Cherokees against the United States, when I was in the War Office, my memory will not enable me to go into detail, and state to you particular circumstances. But I well recollect your many calls upon me in my official capacity, and of the energy and interest with which you pressed upon me those Indian claims. You appeared to me to have paid much attention to the subject, and to be in full possession of a knowledge of their claim, and the facts and arguments upon which it rested. I have the impression, too, that at one time, in your calls upon me, you had with you papers drawn up by yourself, in exposition and in support of those Cherokee claims.

Very respectfully, sir, your obedient servant,

Mr. Kendall. WM. WILKINS.

DEPARTMENT OF THE INTERIOR,
OFFICE INDIAN AFFAIRS, *April* 8, 1852.

SIR: With reference to the letter of the Hon. James Cooper, in which he states that the "Committee on Indian Affairs of the Senate 'desire to know what has been the practice of your Department, during 'and previous to your administration of its affairs, in relation to the 'payment of attorneys' and agents' fees, commissions, &c., for the 'prosecution of Indian and other claims against the United States, and 'what authority for making such payments is recognised as legal by 'the Department," I have the honor to report, that *previous to the 1st of October*, 1846, *as I am informed, the practice of this Office was to allow attorneys and agents representing Indian claims the several amounts contracted to be paid them by the parties whom they represented.* At the period referred to this practice was discontinued, for the reasons assigned in a communication from the Hon. W. L. Marcy, then Secretary of War, addressed to Commissioner Medill, a copy of which is herewith transmitted, for the information of the Committee; and *such amount only has since been allowed attorneys and agents as from the nature of the services rendered, in the judgment of this Office, was conceived "to be a fair and just compensation for their trouble and expense."*

The authority regarded as sufficient in making such payments is a *regular power of attorney*, or instrument in writing, formally executed by claimants, with satisfactory evidence of their identity, and that the paper was fully explained to and understood by them previous to its execution. Very respectfully, your obedient servant,

L. LEA,
Commissioner.

Hon. J. J. CRITTENDEN, *Act'g Sec. Interior.*

www.ingramcontent.com/pod-product-compliance
Lightning Source LLC
LaVergne TN
LVHW011627120826
845150LV00012B/2348

* 9 7 8 1 4 1 8 1 9 4 3 5 2 *